"With her boundless creativity and clear insight into teens' sensibilities, Lisa Schab has given teens an enormous gift—a way into a place where they can be open to, love, and accept themselves wholeheartedly. Grounded in evidence-based practices such as cognitive behavioral therapy (CBT) and dialectical behavior therapy (DBT), *Find Your Self-Love Here* guides teens on a journey of self-reflection and discovery on which they learn to truly embrace who they are. I so wish I had this journal when I was a teen!"

—KAREN BLUTH, PHD, associate professor at the University of North Carolina; and author of several books for teens, including *The Self-Compassion Workbook for Teens*

"By using this transformational journal, readers will find their inner value and accept their authentic selves. Through positive self-talk and learning to acknowledge their special gifts, this journal enables teens to overcome self-doubt and develop self-love. Each turn of the page will make you smile!"

—SALLY WILKINSON, MSW, family therapist for the community support services program at Allendale Association

"*Find Your Self-Love Here* is a warm, inviting, and engaging journal for teens. This is not blank-page journaling which intimidates. Instead, Lisa begins with simple explanations of self-love and then moves into guiding exercises of self-discovery. Each page is a new creative thought exercise. I have used Lisa's journals as resources for adolescents in my medical practice for years. They are gifts on the journey of self-understanding and self-acceptance. This is another gem."

—KATHRYN MILLER, MD, family physician specializing in pediatrics who has practiced at an FQHC on the west side of Chicago for eighteen years

"I have used and loved Lisa Schab's books for years in schools and private practice. This self-love journal is an incredible tool to help adolescents build an authentic and grounded sense of self. Adolescents face so many obstacles to developing a positive identity in the world of social media and instant gratification. The sense of possibility and optimism in this journal makes change and growth feel possible."

—JOLENE FARMER, LCPC, school psychologist in Anne Arundel County Public Schools, licensed clinical professional counselor, and board-approved supervisor in Maryland

"I wish this book had been available when my kids were teens. Lisa makes self-love accessible and engaging, guiding her readers through a fun, practical journey of self-discovery. As an organizational psychologist and business coach, I often see people struggle with self-love later in life. This book is the antidote: a self-hug from start to finish, masterfully weaving facets of our true selves."

—VANESSA CARSTENS, devoted mom, industrial and organizational psychologist, certified business coach, and foresight practitioner at Futures Matter in South Africa

"Lisa Schab has created a valuable resource that can help teens cultivate healthy self-worth. Her creative prompts throughout this journal introduce teens to key concepts that are essential for disrupting negative thought patterns and building self-acceptance. This journal is a timely gift that can counter the unhealthy messages of our digital age and anchor teens with inner resources that can equip them for what lies ahead."

—ASHLEY VIGIL-OTERO, PSYD, clinical psychologist, and co-author of The Self-Confidence Workbook for Teens

"Lisa creatively demonstrates how well of a listener she is with the teens she journeys with in therapy. *Find Your Self-Love Here* offers a supportive invitation for teens to journal while learning the importance of how thinking not only affects our inner dialogue, but how it changes the brain. This journal is a source of hope and encouragement, and provides practical tools in the area of neuroplasticity. Highly recommended!"

—MARSHA THAYER, LICSW, private practice therapist and spiritual director

"Known for her insightful and empathetic approach, Lisa continues to empower young minds with her latest creation. This journal is a transformative journey designed to challenge and inspire teens to truly discover and embrace their authentic selves. Through insightful prompts, reflective exercises, and empowering affirmations, Lisa guides readers to a deeper understanding and appreciation of who they are. This journal is a must-have for any teen seeking to cultivate self-love and confidence in their own unique journey."

—MARK DAVIS, MSW, special programs interventionist at Victor J. Andrew High School

Find Your Self-Love Here

A Creative Journal to Help
Teens Build Confidence &
Embrace Who They Are

Lisa M. Schab, LCSW

INSTANT HELP BOOKS

An Imprint of New Harbinger Publications, Inc.

Publisher's Note

This publication is designed to provide accurate and authoritative information in regard to the subject matter covered. It is sold with the understanding that the publisher is not engaged in rendering psychological, financial, legal, or other professional services. If expert assistance or counseling is needed, the services of a competent professional should be sought.

INSTANT HELP, the Clock Logo, and NEW HARBINGER are trademarks of New Harbinger Publications, Inc.

New Harbinger Publications is an employee-owned company.

Copyright © 2024 by Lisa M. Schab

Instant Help Books
An imprint of New Harbinger Publications, Inc.
5720 Shattuck Avenue
Oakland, CA 94609
www.newharbinger.com

Cover and interior design by Amy Shoup

Acquired by Tesilya Hanauer

Printed in the United States of America

26   25   24

10   9   8   7   6   5   4   3   2   1   First Printing

This book is dedicated to
all the amazing teens who've
let me share bits of their
adolescent journey with them.
May you realize the incredible
value of your authentic self
and watch how it flourishes
when nurtured with self-love!

OPEN
THIS
DOOR

If you want to know . . .

What Self-Love Is . . .

SELF-LOVE is a way of thinking and behaving that stems from a deep knowing that you are a valuable person—and so is everyone else!

SELF-LOVE is the practice of both accepting and celebrating your Authentic Self (who you truly are) and also allowing yourself to glow and grow.

SELF-LOVE is treating yourself with compassion, kindness, patience, caring, gentleness, respect, and all the other qualities you would show your best friend.

People with self-love:

- Understand and believe in their innate value and equality to others

- Focus on their positive attributes

- Enjoy their successes and accept their imperfections

- Stay connected to an inner anchor of peace and balance even when outside circumstances or the opinions of others challenge their confidence

Where Self-Love Comes From . . .

SELF-LOVE comes from what you tell yourself!

(Yes, that's it!)

This is a pretty simple concept and a very achievable goal.
(It is not rocket science.) (Actually, it's neuroscience!)

However, *there is no magic wand.*

Achieving self-love requires *practice.* The practice of working
with your thoughts and changing your brain habits. (Hence,
neuroscience.)

This is exactly what this journal will help you do!

How to Get Self-Love . . .

STEP 1: Understand your intrinsic, unconditional value and worth

Every single infant who enters this world has value and worth.

There has never been an exception.

This includes you!

Seriously. A doctor has never picked up a precious newborn and said, "Oh, too bad, this one has no value." It just doesn't happen!

Important note: Even if you were *not* picked up by a doctor—even if you were born in an alley, abandoned, or abused—it had *nothing* to do with your innate value. That had to do with the problems of the people who created you. It was *not about you.*

The only reason not everyone realizes their innate value is because their brain has received and believed *other* thoughts. Parents, guardians, society, culture, peers, and media all send us messages that affect how we feel about ourselves.

The positive messages create self-love.

The negative messages create self-doubt.

These kinds of messages help **affirm** the truth of our innate value:

"I love you SO much."

"You are a gift in my life."

"You are a miracle."

"You are filled with goodness."

"It's OK if you made a mistake—you're human!"

These kinds of messages **undermine** the truth of our innate value:

"Why are you such a difficult child?"

"It's good to look like this—but not this."

"I wish you were more like them."

"This is how you should be, but you're not."

"You'll never amount to anything."

Do any of these
sound familiar?

(Check or underline
or otherwise mark
them in any way that
feels good.)

STEP 2: Commit to choosing and using positive self-messages

The messages we pay attention to, believe, and repeat become our "self-messages" and they all affect our sense of self-worth. If the messages are positive, we think we have reason to love ourselves. If they are negative, we begin to doubt.

The good news: No matter how long you have listened to or believed negative messages—it's never too late to change! *It is never too late* to start working on what you tell yourself and create self-love.

Because (and here's the neuroscience!) every time you even consider thinking differently, the neural pathways in your brain begin to change. Every time you challenge a negative message, it starts breaking down. Every time you repeat or even consider a positive message, it starts building up. With repetition, over time, your brain becomes wired for self-love!

More good news! Our brains are "plastic." (No, not plastic like shrink-wrap—plastic meaning malleable, and capable of change as long as we are alive.)

SO, even if your brain has received and believed negative thoughts about yourself for a *long time, it can change!*

You can decide to choose and use positive thoughts about yourself.

You can decide to release judgmental thoughts and choose supportive thoughts.

You can decide to stop mean and demeaning self-talk and choose kind and caring self-talk.

This is real and possible!!

And this book gives you page after page of ways to practice.

STEP 3: Discover, accept, and celebrate your Authentic Self

Your Authentic Self is your *true* self. It's who you are before you start believing messages that you're not good enough. It's who you are without trying to be different, look different, or act different because you doubt you have enough value just the way you are.

In reality, your Authentic Self is your best self and will lead you to fulfilling your highest potential. Your Authentic Self embodies your unique talents, skills, gifts, passions, and purpose.

Self-love is created when you explore and discover your Authentic Self, accept whatever you find, and celebrate the amazing being that you are.

It grows and flourishes when you start sending yourself all the positive messages you need and deserve.

STEP 4: Practice and repeat, practice and repeat, practice and repeat

Just like you trained your brain to be able to read, you can train your brain to choose positive messages and release negative messages with practice.

Again, it's *never too late* to turn things around! Even if you've felt unworthy or disliked yourself for a long time, you can start the change at this very moment.

IMPORTANT NOTE: Change is not linear or perfect! Like everything else in life, it's a journey. You won't change your thinking habits overnight. You will have days or weeks when the negative thoughts seem like they've taken over and won. But they haven't! Just by using this journal you've started changing your thinking patterns.

> * AND THE MORE YOU PRACTICE,
> THE BETTER YOU'LL GET!

A FEW TIPS FOR USING THIS JOURNAL

1 The prompts in this journal are designed to help you create self-love by learning to believe in your innate value, discover and accept your Authentic Self, choose and use positive self-messages, and release negative messages.

2 You can complete the prompts in whatever order feels best for you! Trust your Authentic Self to guide you to whatever you need in the moment.

3 You can expand on or shift or wiggle any prompt around to make it work better for you. Feel free to write if it says draw, cut if it says paste, tear out the best pages to tape on your wall, or skip any prompts that just do not work for you.

4 This book is not about a "right way" or a "wrong way" or any other rules that trigger you to judge yourself. You don't have to be a great (or even mediocre!) writer or artist to use these prompts to give your brain practice changing from self-doubt to self-love.

If you notice that you're judging
yourself as you go along—
that's OK! Just notice it,
breathe, smile, and let it go!
Love yourself for being on
the journey!

Sit comfortably... shoulders relaxed... smile... take a breath.
Feel your heart opening to the idea of loving yourself.

Write - draw - color your intention here...

I accept who I am.

I SEE ALL MY GOOD.

I forgive myself.

I cherish every
part of me.

I open my heart to myself.

Dear Self,

I am tired of disliking you, being mean to you, and talking down to you! You deserve better! I am breaking up with Self-Doubt and starting a new relationship with Self-Love. I want you to know...

Love, _____

Without thinking
too much, (circle)
the item in each
pair that appeals
to you the most.

WALK / RIDE

cook / eat out

WRITE / SPEAK

focus / dream

BOOKS / TV

HOME / AWAY

PLANE / CAR

hard / soft

bath / shower

FAST / SLOW

FORMAL / CASUAL

meat / veggies

DARK / LIGHT

COMEDY / DRAMA

COLA / CLEAR

alone / together

sandals / sneakers

CURLY / STRAIGHT

save / discard

COLD / HOT

NUMBERS / WORDS

DAY / NIGHT

desert / mountains

GIVE / RECEIVE

ROCK / RAP

school / work

AIR / GROUND

jeans / sweats

SUGAR / SALT

CITY / COUNTRY

structure / flow

SPRING / FALL

land / sea

play / watch

SITCOM / NEWS

talk / listen

Add any comments you'd like!

17

Is there any part of you that's hesitant about self-love?
(That's normal and OK! Let yourself feel it, let it out here,
and then move on...)

What are you afraid might happen if you try loving yourself?

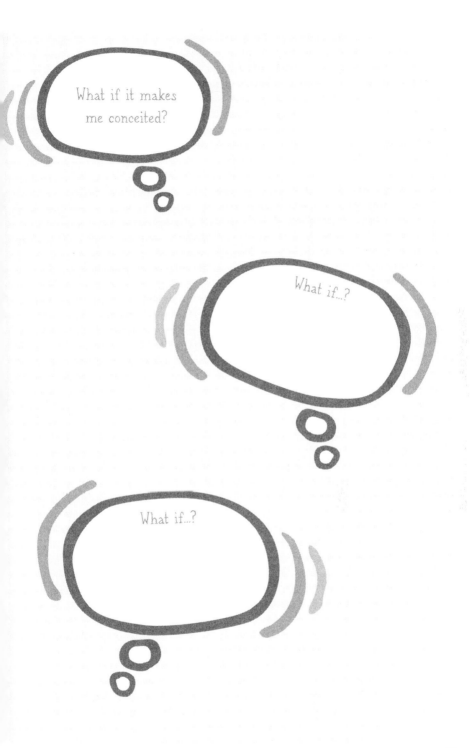

19

Who sent you the message that you weren't good enough?
Write them a letter here, explaining **how wrong they were**.

IF THERE WERE NO ONE TO JUDGE OR CRITICIZE ME...

I would wear...

I would be...

I would say...

I would do...

I would decide...

I would be friends with...

GR♡TITUDE ALPHABET!

Everything from A to Z that's good about me

(from A—my Ankles work ... to L—I like to Laugh ... to Zzz—I'm a great sleeper!)

A

B

C

D

E

F

G

H

I

J

K

L

M

N

O

P

Q

R

S

T

U

V

W

X

Y

Z

There is absolutely nothing you can do, get, or accomplish that could make you any worthier of goodness than you are at this exact moment... Take a deep breath and let that sink in. You are enough, exactly as you are.

—PANACHE DESAI

Help your brain accept this new perspective.

Write yourself a permission slip to love yourself.

(This is your)

PERMISSION SLIP

_____

_____

_____

_____

_____

_____

♥ _____

IMAGINE IT'S THE FIRST DAY OF YOUR LIFE!

In each box, write or draw what you would give as gifts to your amazing newborn infant self. Choose from the list below or write your own.

SELF-ACCEPTANCE...SELF-COMPASSION...LIGHTHEARTEDNESS...POSITIVITY...

JOY...SENSE OF HUMOR...SELF-WORTH...INNER PEACE...CONFIDENCE...LOVE

50 WAYS ♥

TO LOVE YOUR BODY, MIND, AND SPIRIT

Circle those you like or add more.

forgive yourself

let yourself play

wear soft socks

let someone you trust
give you a back rub

practice honesty

let yourself dream

use soothing lotion

take a nap

face your fears

take a breath

put on headphones
and drift away

take a walk

believe in something

strive for balance

wear clothes you love

pace yourself

believe you can

set realistic goals

sing

read something you love

ask for help

tell someone your problem

sip something that
makes you smile

embrace your imperfection

let yourself cry

gently stretch out
your tension

watch a video that makes
you laugh out loud

dance

focus on the good

massage your toes

take a break

dwell on a favorite
memory

listen to your
intuition

write in a journal

eat when you're
hungry

stop rushing

stare at the sky

eat your favorite
meal

go outside

imagine you can fly

be with people who
build you up

speak kindly to
yourself

enjoy the present
moment

set healthy boundaries
with people

be open to possibilities

move your body

get lost in a hobby

eat fruits and veggies

brush your hair

keep an open mind

Nourish yourself with at least one a day.

Write the beginning of a story about someone starting on the path to self-love. Write the end of the story where they're living in self-love. Then fill in their journey. How do they get there?

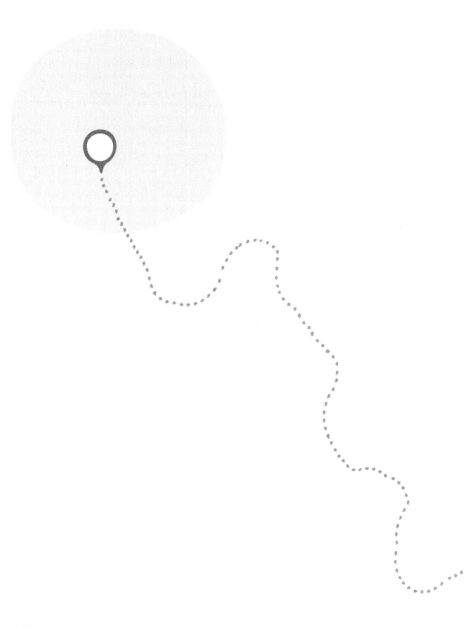

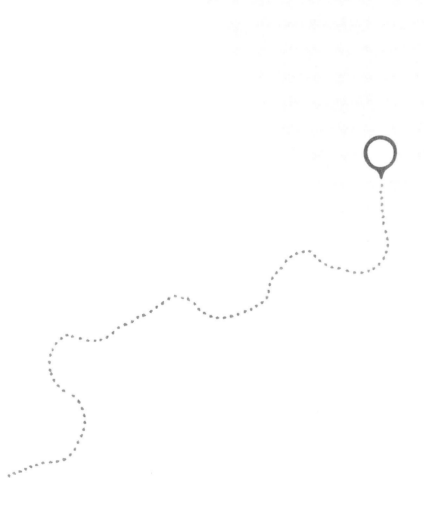

IS THERE ANYTHING YOU HIDE IN TO AVOID SELF-LOVE?

staying too busy

other people

overworking

sports

social media

overstudying

drugs

drinking

WHAT DOES IT
FEEL LIKE TO
RISK COMING OUT
OF HIDING?

CREATE A WORD PORTRAIT OF YOUR AUTHENTIC SELF.

Write or arrange as many adjectives as you can to describe who you are when you're being The Real You.

(Tip: A thesaurus can help!)

Colors... words... pictures... designs... textures... lines... souvenirs ----

-------------------- > <u>Saturate these collage pages with self-love!</u>

What do you need to hear more of? (What messages would you love to receive from other people, society, or the universe?)

Write these messages as if you're saying them to yourself!
Use your name.

Fill these pages with as many of your successes as you can fit.
(Learn to walk? Learn to read? Make a friend? Pass a class? Make a team? Throw a great party?)

BASK in the glow!

If I could create and experience
ANY FUTURE I WANTED, I would...

My dreams lead me to my authentic self. ♥

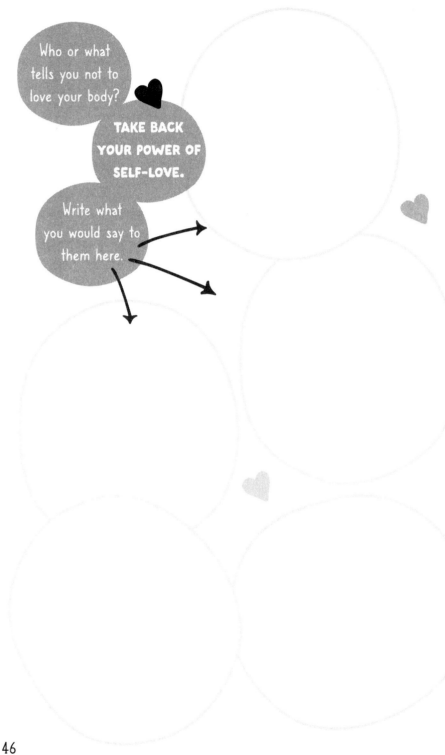

Who or what tells you not to love your body?

TAKE BACK YOUR POWER OF SELF-LOVE.

Write what you would say to them here.

Describe 3 things you would do today
if you already felt SERIOUS Self-Love...

1. _____

2. _____

3. _____

Choose one and
do it now!

1. WRITE THAT THING YOU REGRET HERE.

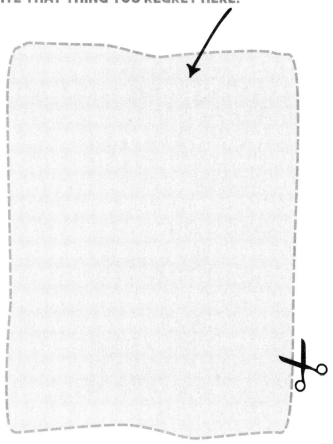

2. CUT IT OUT AND DESTROY IT.

3. FORGIVE YOURSELF AND START FRESH!

It's not just you! People from every corner of the world need love. Write the word "self-love" in as many languages as you can find... feel, draw, describe your union with everyone.

51

Fill in each blank with your name.

⭐ You don't have to believe it right away.

⭐ You don't have to be comfortable with it right away.

⭐ Just give it a try and let your brain absorb the idea.

_____, I love you.

_____, you're good enough.

_____, you're amazing.

_____,
you're a valuable person.

_____, I care about you.

⭐ Write more of your own.

_____,

_____

_____.

_____,

_____

_____.

_____,

_____

_____.

53

LISTENING TO YOUR **AUTHENTIC SELF,**
IDENTIFY WHAT YOU VALUE.

Rate each of these on a 1 (low) to 10 (high) scale according to
how much each one means to you:

_____ family

_____ romantic relationships

_____ friendships

_____ work

_____ education/training

_____ recreation/fun

_____ spirituality

_____ citizenship/community life

_____ physical self-care

_____ emotional self-care

_____ environmental concerns

_____ art/creative expression

_____ other _____

_____ other _____

Tell why...

↑

Scroll social media
for 15 minutes and
pay attention to
the thoughts that
enter your mind.

Record them here.
Circle those that make
you feel good about
yourself. Cross out
those that make you
feel like you're not
good enough.

↓

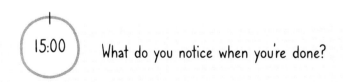

15:00 What do you notice when you're done?

TRY A SELF-LOVE MOMENT

Find a place you feel safe.

Sit quietly and comfortably and close your eyes or lower your gaze.

Notice your breath and gently invite it to relax your body and mind.

As you inhale and exhale, invite yourself to be only your true self.

Let ideas of who you *think* you have to be or should be simply float away and disappear.

For this moment you are only your Authentic Self.

As you breathe, feel the peace and joy of this state.

Imagine self-love flowing through every cell, every muscle, and every organ of your body.

Imagine only self-love flowing through your mind and spirit.

Stay with this for as long as you feel comfortable.

Then write or draw.

(Anything safe!) New flavor? New song? New hair?
New app? New color?

Important Note: The outcome doesn't matter.

Write about your experience and your ability to
open... expand... and grow.

Write all the mean,
negative things you say to
or about yourself here:

Now tear out
this page and
shred it!

Draw or describe your **INNER ANCHOR OF SELF-LOVE** that is unchangeable no matter what tides of circumstance or opinion arise.

> I refuse to believe that the processed beauty
> that I see around me is what I have to be.
> —RAE SMITH

AN IMPOSSIBLE BEAUTY IDEAL makes a lot of money for people in the beauty industry, and it simultaneously crushes everyone's self-esteem.

Create a new "looks" business that would promote self-acceptance, self-love, and build people up. Mission plan... products... goals...?

Love-Your-Looks Business

MISSION PLAN...?   PRODUCTS...?   GOALS...?

Write your name...

○ upside down

○ backwards

○ out inside

○ **IN BOLD LETTERS**

○ *ON A SLANT*

○ IN A CIRCLE

○ **inaknot**

○ in a different color

○ *in a curly font*

○ **in a scary font**

○ in a mysterious font

○ *IN YOUR FAVORITE FONT*

○ on a different page

○ any other way you want!

THE POSSIBILITIES OF YOU ARE ENDLESS!

66

Think of a time when you felt unloved as a child. Maybe someone criticized you, hurt you, or abandoned you. Write a caring letter from yourself today to your younger self using words of love and compassion and kindness. Tell your younger self all the things you needed to hear but didn't when that happened.

Dear Younger Self,

Read it out loud to yourself now.

TATTOO?

EARRING?

HAIRSTYLE?

Show or describe the body art
that feels just right for you...

DESCRIBE YOUR FRIENDSCAPE

I express and love my Authentic Self when I'm with

_____

Because... _____

_____

_____

_____

_____

I express and love my Authentic Self when I'm with

_____

Because... _____

_____

_____

_____

_____

I feel down on myself or reject who I really am when I'm with

_____

Because... _____

_____

_____

_____

_____

I feel down on myself or reject who I really am when I'm with

_____

Because... _____

_____

_____

_____

_____

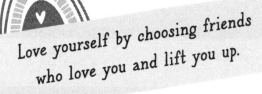

Love yourself by choosing friends
who love you and lift you up.

73

START YOUR SELF-L♥VE

"

"

"

"

QUOTE*COLLECTION HERE.

"

"

"

"

* Include any thoughts, phrases, or ideas that help you
LOVE, **ACCEPT**, or **CELEBRATE** your Authentic Self.

Help your brain practice nonjudgment!

Spend the next hour or day *observing* yourself and your life instead of judging them. Notice and record thoughts, feelings, events, people, situations, and behaviors. When judgment thoughts come in (as they will!) note them here and then practice gently letting them go. *Accept* however this feels.

77

My best friend:

Things I SAY
to show them love:

Things I DO
to show them love:

When and how can I say and do these same things for <u>MYSELF</u>?

In ancient times it was believed there was a vein running from our fourth finger to our heart. This finger became associated with love and thus, the home for engagement and wedding rings.

Trace your hand here.

✦ Design and draw a ring on your ring finger that represents your new commitment to self-love.

IF YOU WERE TO THROW YOUR AUTHENTIC SELF **THE BEST PARTY EVER,** WHAT WOULD IT LOOK LIKE?

DECORATIONS

MUSIC

GUEST LIST

FOOD

WHAT ELSE??

83

When we experience LOVE we feel joyful -
peaceful - open - and safe.

Name any **places** - **people**
- or **situations** that bring
these feelings to you.

Describe the ways you can
bring them to yourself.

TODAY'S EXPERIMENT:

Every time you notice
you're feeling bad about
yourself because of
something on social
media, turn off your
device for 30 minutes.

* What is it like to unhook?

_____

_____

_____

_____

_____

_____

_____

* Describe whether or how social media affects your self-messages...

Plan and carry out a

SELF-LOVE DAY!

(By yourself or with a friend.)

What will you do for your body?

What will you do for your mind?

What will you do for your spirit?

A "RIGHT" WAY TO LOOK IS COMPLETELY SUBJECTIVE.

If you ran the planet, what messages would you send people of all shapes, sizes, and colors to help them love and accept their bodies?

THE SONG LYRICS THAT MAKE YOU FEEL REALLY CONFIDENT:

Highlight the best lines.
Say them out loud.
Rewrite them everywhere!

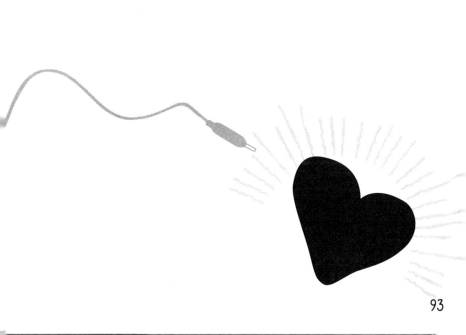

My AUTHENTIC SELF believes that...

I have a right to my beliefs.

DWELL ON YOUR POSITIVES INSTEAD OF YOUR NEGATIVES!

Write them… draw them… doodle them… ponder them…

Come back and dwell here again and again!

THESE PEOPLE WILL BE STUDIED AND REMEMBERED FOR GENERATIONS TO COME.

- Martin Luther King, Jr.
- Abraham Lincoln
- Albert Einstein
- Mahatma Gandhi
- Amelia Earhart
- Nelson Mandela
- William Shakespeare
- Mother Teresa
- Thomas Edison
- Eleanor Roosevelt
- Marie Curie
- Rosa Parks
- Maya Angelou
- Galileo
- Leonardo da Vinci
- Anne Frank

Circle those whose contributions to society had anything to do with the way they looked.

DESCRIBE WHAT *YOU* WANT TO CONTRIBUTE TO THE WORLD...

I am good enough.

I DID GREAT
YESTERDAY.

I BELIEVE IN ME.

On each sticky note,
write a self-affirmation
that lifts you up. Cut them
out and place them around
your life (locker? mirror?
wallet? car?) as gifts
to yourself.

Yes, I can!

Dear Self,
you are
awesome!

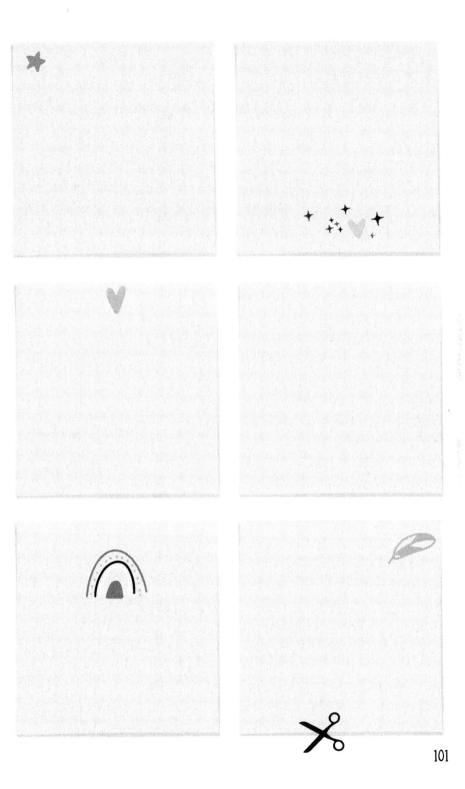

You are a child of the universe,

no less than the trees and the stars;

you have a right to be here...

—MAX EHRMANN

Design a video game specifically for you.

♥ The starting level is the self-love you have now.
♥ The final level is the self-love you're looking for.
♥ Think about your: environment... characters...
storyline... challenges... rewards... art
and graphics... music...

I have the right to say NO.

I take care of myself by setting healthy boundaries with these people...

107

CELEBRATE YOUR BODY!

No matter what it has *looked* like, list the gifts
your body has given you during your lifetime.
(Running? Hugging? Tasting chocolate? Watching a sunset?
Playing ball? Swimming? Kissing? Hearing music?)

_____

_____

_____

_____

_____

_____

_____

_____

_____

★ _____
★ _____
★ _____
★ _____
★ _____
★ _____
★ _____
★ _____
★ _____
★ _____
★ _____

> The reason we struggle with insecurity is because we compare our behind-the-scenes with everyone else's highlight reel.
> —STEVEN FURTICK

WHOSE LIFE DO YOU THINK LOOKS SO MUCH BETTER THAN YOURS?

REFRAME YOUR PERSPECTIVE AND IMAGINE THEIR BEHIND-THE-SCENES REEL.

What might they not share?

_____

_____

_____

_____

_____

What challenges might they have that you don't see? _____

_____

_____

_____

What might be their inner fears, insecurities, or doubts? (_Everyone has these!_) _____

_____

_____

_____

_____

Ask a few people you trust what they **LOVE** about you. Stuff these pillows with their words! Read them over when you're feeling self-doubt and allow them to cushion you.

113

Fill these pages with whatever feels good right now.
Listen to your **Authentic Self** for direction.
(You can't do it wrong!)

Notice items that make you feel **GOOD** about yourself.

List them here and then move them to a place of prominence.

Notice items that make you feel **BAD** about yourself.

List them here and then move them out.

How does this feel?

SELF-LOVE BEGINS WITH A SMALL VOICE DEEP WITHIN YOU.

- When you make a mistake, it says,

  "It doesn't matter, you're human."

- When you feel self-doubt, it says,

  "It's OK, you're <u>absolutely</u> good enough."

- When you notice your imperfections, it says,

  "I accept you exactly the way you are."

LET YOUR SELF-LOVE VOICE SPEAK HERE...

I AM...

VALUABLE

EXTRAORDINARY

A MASTERPIECE

WORTHY

JUST RIGHT

UNIQUE

GOOD ENOUGH

*(Repeat to yourself as you
relax, breathe, and color!)*

Name something about yourself you previously
thought was unlovable. Write it here.

- -

Now sit quietly,
close your eyes,
and take a deep, peaceful breath.
Open your mind and your heart.

Imagine loving this part of yourself.
It doesn't have to make sense or feel real—just go with it.
See yourself accepting and loving this part of you
with all your heart, as if you've found a lost puppy.

Embrace it physically and emotionally.
Send it words of love.
Keep breathing with kindness and empathy.

When you're done, write or draw. ⟶

The Miraculous

PLAINS OF PHYSICAL STRENGTHS

- _____
- _____
- _____
- _____

MOUNTAINS OF MENTAL STRENGTHS

- _____
- _____
- _____
- _____

Land of Me

SEAS OF SPIRITUAL STRENGTHS

- _____
- _____
- _____
- _____

RIVERS OF EMOTIONAL STRENGTHS

- _____
- _____
- _____
- _____

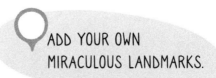

ADD YOUR OWN
MIRACULOUS LANDMARKS.

YOUR TRUTH
ISN'T
ABOUT WHAT OTHER PEOPLE DO, THINK, OR SAY.

YOUR TRUTH
COMES FROM
YOUR DEEP INNER AUTHENTIC SELF.

WHO DO YOU WANT TO BE IN THE UNIVERSE?
HOW WILL THIS GUIDE YOUR CHOICES?

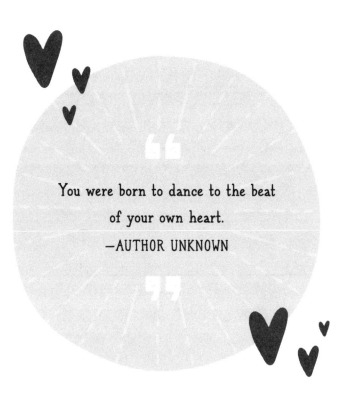

You were born to dance to the beat
of your own heart.

—AUTHOR UNKNOWN

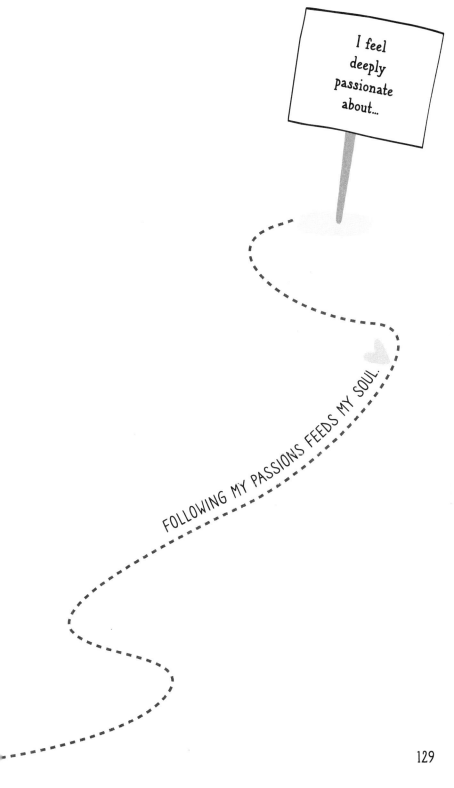

I feel deeply passionate about...

FOLLOWING MY PASSIONS FEEDS MY SOUL.

Create an ad or meme that would help young children love themselves.

YOU'VE JUST MOVED INTO YOUR OWN APARTMENT WITH AN UNLIMITED BUDGET.

 SHOW THE FLOOR PLAN THAT'S PERFECT FOR YOU.

HOW DO YOU DECORATE IT?

 WHAT DO YOU FILL IT WITH TO REFLECT ONLY YOUR AUTHENTIC SELF?

LOVE YOURSELF WITH **ALL YOUR SENSES!**

What feels SO good to you?

SOUNDS...

SMELLS...

TASTES...

SIGHTS...

TEXTURES...

Practice giving yourself some of these every day.

ACTING ASSERTIVELY

MEANS
"STANDING UP
FOR YOURSELF
WHILE ALSO
RESPECTING
THE RIGHTS
OF OTHERS."

WHAT'S HAPPENING
IN YOUR LIFE
RIGHT NOW WHERE
YOU COULD
PRACTICE
SELF-LOVE
BY ACTING
ASSERTIVELY?

REHEARSE
IT HERE
WITH WORDS
OR PICTURES...

What do you wear to totally relax?

Not for fashion or to "be seen"!

Put on these clothes and write or draw about this act of self-love

—or anything else—from your chill comfort zone.

Your feelings stem from your **Authentic Self** and you have a right to all of them.

With love and acceptance, tell what each of these bring up for you (or add your own).

LOVE

Envy

ANXIETY

Joy

contentment

fear

IRRITATION

DISAPPOINTMENT

peace

ANGER

GRATITUDE

EXCITEMENT

GUILT

HAPPINESS

PLEASURE

CONFUSION

embarrassment

PRIDE

WHO HELPS YOU FEEL GOOD ABOUT YOU?

What would they tell you if you were feeling down on yourself?

Write their words here...

TAKE A PICTURE
OF THIS PAGE AND
REREAD IT
WHENEVER YOU
NEED IT.

Choose from these words (or write your own) and finish the sentence.

CONFIDENT

BEAUTIFUL

STRONG

LOVABLE

UNIQUE

TALENTED

AMAZING

CREATIVE

SMART

I AM...

Tear out this page and slip it under your mattress. Seriously—do it! Let these words infuse your mind every night as you fall asleep.

CELEBRATE THE
PERFECTION OF YOUR IMPERFECTION!

Describe a mistake you once made that
actually led to something wonderful.

UNCONDITIONAL LOVE means being loved and accepted at every moment *just because you are here, no matter what.* (Not because you did or didn't do something or think something or say something or become something.)

Set the intention to love yourself unconditionally. Write it here. Decorate the page from your heart.

<u>*TAPE HERE*</u> *A PICTURE OF YOURSELF THAT YOU LOVE*

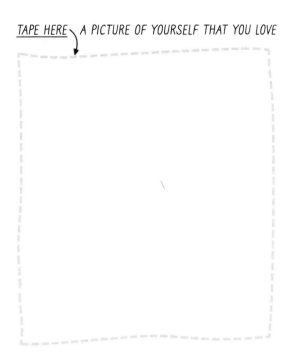

<u>*TAPE HERE*</u> *A PICTURE OF YOURSELF THAT YOU THOUGHT YOU COULDN'T LOVE*

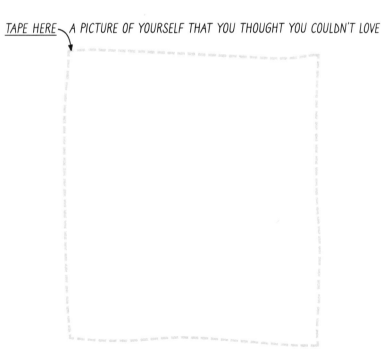

Describe the deep inner value of you that is unchangeable no matter how you look at any moment.

Try to feel
unconditional love
for YOU.
♥

_____
_____
_____
_____
_____
_____
_____
_____
_____
_____
_____
_____
_____
_____
_____
_____
_____

Love
yourself for
trying.
♥

151

Loving yourself... frees, uplifts

What can you become?

and expands you.

How you once defined yourself through the
eyes of **NEGATIVITY**:

How you define yourself now through
the eyes of **SELF-LOVE**:

Write a

NEW TITLE

and design a

NEW COVER

for this book,

making it a

perfect match

for your

AUTHENTIC SELF.

Write the date for

ONE YEAR FROM NOW

....

♥

WHAT WILL YOU BE DOING DIFFERENTLY THAT REFLECTS YOUR NEW STATE OF SELF-LOVE?

....

....

....

159

WHAT
TO DO
NEXT

1. CONGRATULATE YOURSELF!

If you've opened or read or completed any part of this book, you've taken a step toward self-love.

Just allowing yourself to *consider* self-love starts your brain on the track to healing, growth, and positive change!

You've planted a seed, and now, if you decide to keep practicing, that seed can grow.

A nice act of self-love would be to let yourself share, honestly— from your Authentic Self—anything you're thinking or feeling right now, and to *accept* whatever that is...

2. Practice...

Go back and look at the introduction to this book again. Underline, highlight, circle, star, or mark any ideas that you really want to remember. Make a copy and put them where you can see and read them first thing every morning. Let them grow roots deep into your brain until they become automatic background thoughts that follow you everywhere.

3. Look ahead...

Think about where you want to go with self-love from here. Have you had enough? Do you need a break from thinking about it? Or are you hungry for a bit more?

(There is no right or wrong answer. Wherever you are on the self-love journey is OK!)

4. Journey gently...

Wherever you go from here, wherever your path takes you, try to be gentle with yourself.

> Loving the self, to me, begins with
> never ever criticizing ourselves for anything.... .
> Criticism locks us into the very pattern we are trying
> to change. Understanding and being gentle with ourselves
> helps us to move out of it. Remember, you have been
> criticizing yourself for years and it hasn't worked.
> Try approving of yourself and see what happens.
> —LOUISE HAY

NOTE TO PARENTS, PROFESSIONALS, AND ANYONE CARING FOR A TEEN

Find Your Self-Love Here offers over 80 journaling prompts designed specifically to help teens realize their innate value, discover and embrace their authentic selves, and change their neural patterns from a negative self-view to positivity and self-love. Working with the prompts helps readers practice this *in the moment* as well as over time. Creative, engaging, and clinically based, these prompts are grounded in the principles of cognitive behavioral therapy, dialectical behavior therapy, mindfulness-based therapies, and neuroscience.

This journal can be used by a teen on their own or as an adjunct to counseling or psychotherapy. It lends itself to both individual and group settings and can help the average adolescent as well as the hard-to-reach teen and those uncomfortable with traditional talk therapy.

Where direct questioning and exploration might feel threatening, journaling prompts are more subtle and can bypass defenses. When used at times of self-doubt, the journal can help teens interrupt the habitual thought cycle, decrease negativity, and shift to positive self-talk. The prompts are designed to help teens start dismantling negative self-messages and build new neural pathways for self-love through cognitive restructuring, visualization, meditation, mind-body awareness, self-soothing, and self-expression. Creative prompts help teens raise their self-awareness and develop self-acceptance and self-compassion while still maintaining comfort with the process.

For a clinical guide to using this book specifically, and journaling as an adjunct to therapy in general, please visit http://www.lisamschabooks.com. Alternatively, you can visit http://www.53922 and follow the instructions there to register your book and download the companion guide. If you are interested in earning continuing education credits for Lisa Schab's courses on journaling as an adjunct to therapy, please visit https://www.pdresources.org.

Acknowledgments

I am sincerely grateful to the following people who have helped bring this book to life:

Tesilya Hanauer and Madison Davis, who are always respectful, professional, and gentle with my writing, and who continue to present me with opportunities to create.

Amy Shoup and Sara Christian, who give my written words depth, reality, magic, and spirit through their visual artistry.

Amy Blue, Research Queen, who keeps it all honest.

Everyone at New Harbinger who plays a role in this book's production from start to finish and beyond.

Lucy Lucia and Michael Krajovic, who shared their professional wisdom on self-love.

♥

Lisa M. Schab, LCSW, is a practicing psychotherapist in the greater Chicago, IL, area; and author of twenty self-help books, including *The Anxiety Workbook for Teens*, *The Self-Esteem Workbook for Teens*, and the teen guided journals, *Put Your Worries Here* and *Put Your Feelings Here*. She has been interviewed as an expert on Milwaukee television stations WTMJ-TV and WISN-TV, by *The New York Times*, *Scholastic Choices* magazine, *Teen Vogue*, *Psych Central*, and Kate Shannon's *Creative Therapy Umbrella* podcast. Schab has authored regular mental health columns for *Chicago Parent Magazine* and *The Sun* newspapers. She is a member of the National Association of Social Workers (NASW) and the Society of Children's Book Writers and Illustrators (SCBWI).

More ⏱Instant Help Books for Teens

An Imprint of New Harbinger Publications

THE SELF-ESTEEM HABIT FOR TEENS

50 Simple Ways to Build Your Confidence Every Day

978-1626259195 / US $23.95

THE TEEN GIRL'S SURVIVAL JOURNAL

Your Space to Learn, Reflect, Explore, and Take Charge of Your Mental Health

978-1648482861 / US $18.95

THE GIRL'S GUIDE TO RELATIONSHIPS, SEXUALITY, AND CONSENT

Tools to Help Teens Stay Safe, Empowered, and Confident

978-1684039739 / US $19.95

THE TEEN BREAKUP SURVIVAL GUIDE

Skills to Help You Deal with Intense Emotions, Cultivate Self-Love, and Come Back with Confidence

978-1648483325 / US $19.95

PUT YOUR WORRIES HERE

A Creative Journal for Teens with Anxiety

978-1684032143 / US $18.95

JUST AS YOU ARE

A Teen's Guide to Self-Acceptance and Lasting Self-Esteem

978-1626255906 / US $17.95

🌼 **newharbinger**publications

1-800-748-6273 / newharbinger.com

(VISA, MC, AMEX / prices subject to change without notice)   Follow Us 📷 📘 𝕏 ▶ 📌 in ♪ ⓖ

Don't miss out on new books from New Harbinger.
Subscribe to our email list at **newharbinger.com/subscribe** 🖱